PAPER BIRDS

Delaina J. Miller
Rosemary Nissen-Wade
Helen Patrice
Leigh D.C. Spencer

Paper Birds © 2025 by Delaina J. Miller, Rosemary Nissen-Wade, Helen Patrice, and Leigh D.C. Spencer

Published by Content X Design, Inc.
Overland Park, KS

All rights reserved.

First Edition

Cover art: *No Woman Is an Island* by Jeanie Tomanek
Cover design: Allison Pang
Book design: Allison Pang
Editor: Carina Bissett

Printed in the United States of America
ISBN: 978-1-942005-61-2
Library of Congress Control Number: 2025930201

Also by Delaina J. Miller, Rosemary Nissen-Wade, Helen Patrice, and Leigh D.C. Spencer

She Too: Four Voices in (Almost) Harmony

Foreword

Back in 2014, four poets reached across continents and oceans to celebrate their love of poetry. Each day during the month of April (National Poetry Month in the United States), these women joined countless others in taking inspiration from daily prompts offered by Robert Lee Brewer at the Poem A Day (PAD) challenge at *Writer's Digest* and NaPoWriMo, an independent project created by Maine poet Maureen Thorson. At the end of the project, the four women—Delaina J. Miller, Helen Patrice, Leigh D.C. Spencer, and Rosemary Nissen-Wade—collected their work in the powerful book *She Too: Four Voices in (Almost) Harmony*.

Time passed. Life went on. But through the years, the connections between these women grew stronger. And so, as the ten-year anniversary of their first collaborative work grew closer, the conversation turned towards remembrance, and then eventually moved to a proposal: the creation of a new book, once again inspired by prompts issued during the month of April. The result is the book you hold in your hands—*Paper Birds*.

The relationships behind this collaboration run deep, yet these women are as unique in their lives as they are in the way they each approach their work. The two Australians, Rosemary and Helen, first met in 1988. The Americans, Delaina and Leigh, originally connected twenty years later in 2008. Over the years, more associations were made, and by 2011 the conversation pathways between the four poets became complete. They successfully created bridges—between cultures and conventions—to become a powerhouse of diverse voices. And what voices they have!

It might seem an impossible task to take a wide array of poems—

written from no less than sixty prompts!—and blend them into a cohesive book. Yet, they've now successfully done it—twice! In this newest collaboration, the pieces work together in often unexpected and engaging ways. For instance, Helen's contemplative insight into the life of her adult autistic son in "Super" offers a much different perspective than Leigh's remembrance of her Jewish son's twenty-first birthday in "Stereotypes." In another example, Rosemary takes readers into the past with a romantic reminiscence of the beginning of a love affair in "The Song, 'Suzanne.'" The continuation of the musical theme of memory appears again, as Delaina travels even further back in time with a tribute to the enduring love of her in-laws—both now suffering from dementia—in "A Soundtrack of Courtship."

Indeed, the musicality of these poems cannot be denied. This is true whether they are written within the constraints of traditional poetic forms or within the looser formatting afforded by free verse. And throughout it all, each poet's voice remains distinct. This can also be seen in presentation as both Rosemary and Helen write using British English, whereas Delaina and Leigh rely on American English conventions when it comes to spelling and grammar. These distinctions have been kept in place, as these poets share the belief that no voice should be forced to conform. And what could be more powerful than that?

Within these pages, you will discover love and loss, triumphs and tragedies. You'll find hope in the magic of rainbows and scenery charted on a map of gratitude, contemplation on climate change and the savagery of genocide, reflections on suicidal ideation and survival in the face of domestic abuse, and the wonder of childhood scavenger hunts and narwhal pajamas. For how else can it be? These women live life to the fullest, and they have been blessed with the power of poetry to share their stories with others. *Paper Birds* presents those stories—a conversation between four women that continues to cross continents and navigate oceans in an (almost) harmonic convergence of poetic brilliance.

—Carina Bissett, award-winning editor, author, and poet

'Hope' is the thing with feathers.

—Emily Dickinson

Contents

Not 'Summertime' but Autumn's 'September Song'	1
At the Very Most	3
Divining Rod	4
Bricks in a Wall	8
The Shadows Dance Upon the Wall (Cento)	10
As a Caregiver, I Learn to Lie Better	14
Eclipse	16
The Sad Anniversaries	18
Comet	20
Smoggy Day/Starry Night	21
Let's Hear It for Elvis!	27
Lunch with Lewis Capaldi	28
I Couldn't Fall in Love with Aquaman	32
Steam and Succour	34
Longing	35
A Soundtrack of Courtship	36
The Song, 'Suzanne'	38
His Blue-Eyed Gal	40
Torment	42
Sustainable	44
On Being Asked to Tell a Tall Tale and Make It Funny	47
Man vs Bear	48
Setting the Bar	50
The New Proust Questionnaire	51
Conflict	52
Poetic Devices Take a Stand	53
Tell-Tale Cliches for Caregivers	54
Stims	56
The Middle of Me	58
The Promise that Never Came True	59

Melt	60
Some Days/Other Days	62
A Metaphor of Donuts	66
Beat Figuratively, Mostly	67
In Media Res	70
Return Me	73
Not All Is Lost	74
Figs	76
Observing Poppi	78
As I Move Nearer	79
The Living Treasures of Memories	80
A Surreal Day	83
Hero	84
The Dream Maker	86
Mysterious Underworld	87
Hercules in the Sauna	88
Arguing with the Nature Spirits	90
The Starry Night Wikipedia Entry	92
The Rattlesnake	94
Haiku Corner	95
A Fisherman's Tale	96
Tell Me a Story	97
Stamps of the World	100
Rumpelmayer's	101
Wondrous Things, Rainbows	105
Talking with the Dead	106
A Remix of Gratitude	109
Mini-Mum	110
Stereotypes	112
The Mordialloc Fairies – A True Story	114
Shades of Purple	116
A Painted Shock to the Senses	117
Can You Keep a Secret?	118
Haunted	120
Communication Breakdowns and Other Caregiver Pitfalls	122
Luck Is Not Chance	123
Do Better	124
Firewalking	126

Incandescent / Until Burnt Out	127
Your Favorite Quote and the Long Goodbye	128
Grilled Cheese & Narwhals	130
Little Lonsdale Street	132
An Atlas of Gratitude	133
When and Where Was I Happiest?	134
This Is Really Living!	136
Learning to Swear Better	138
Unlikely Chapters	140
Not Too Late	142
Hex Value #ece63d	144
Security	146
Historic Event	148
At Least	149
Not My Dog	150
Why I Like Living	154
The Silence Death Leaves	156
The Cage	158
Pause Death	160
The Prompts that Started It All	162
Acknowledgements	168
About the Poet: Delaina J. Miller	170
About the Poet: Rosemary Nissen-Wade	171
About the Poet: Helen Patrice	172
About the Poet: Leigh D.C. Spencer	173

Not 'Summertime' but Autumn's 'September Song'

Rosemary Nissen-Wade

I was going to say something about how the parental promises
in 'Summertime' are lies; because living is never easy, not
for anyone. But then I remember the children in Gaza,
and I decide I can't really complain. I thought to point out
my days dwindle down, but then I recall I've had eighty-four years.

And I remember the children in Gaza, and in other places too,
who don't get to live many days at all, and for whom that living
is brutal, shocking, agonised, insane. And I think that whatever
I've endured (and there have been some things) in the face
of all that, I have suffered nothing. Grief, pain, but no horrors.

There are truths which defeat even poetry. Which even song
can't adequately reflect. Picasso's *Guernica* might come
closer, but I'm a painter in words, and they fail me. Meanwhile
threats of both flooding and fire repeat daily around me.
I can't even think it's peaceful and safe here in my own country.

I lived, I perceive, through a sometime summertime,
when the fish were sometimes jumping – right into the boat
from the lines we trailed. Where we grew no cotton, but
the sun was often high, benignly. I see that my autumn days
are dwindling peacefully and comfortably, precious enough.

The poem has nowhere else to go, yet I don't want to end
on even a weak, qualified high note. To count my blessings
feels detached, isolated, selfish, wilfully blind. With no end
in sight (except the end of the planet), I let it peter out
in a mess of confusion, incomplete, unresolved ...

At the Very Most

Delaina J. Miller

Begin
     breathe
     stride
         again.

Create
     story
     legacy
         repeat.

Thrive
     grow
     evolve
         ignite.

Love
     entirely
     authentically
         Always.

Divining Rod

Leigh D.C. Spencer

What is the name
for this
emotion?

The one where
you're definitely going to
cry, but you
hold it back

A precision
in strangulation

Why?

Why
what?

Why
is the deluge gathering
at all?

Or

Why
bother
holding it back?

I need
to know
if this pending
catharsis
is justified

Or just another
silly
woman
thing

How strong
do I have to be?

Before I dissolve?

I will not
cry
because
you hurt
my feeling
(just the one)

But what if
that fraction
of a fissure
spiderwebbed?

Pointed perfect patterns
across the fluctuating
market value
of my self-worth

Did I consent to this?

Should I?

WHY
is there no seat
at your table
for me

when you
invited me
to come?

Maybe
it's not you
at all

My path itself
is uneven

Pebble teeth nip
but wordless
so I can't tell

Are the skinned knees
of my ego a challenge
or a warning?

Is this path
even for me?

I read a poem today
it made me cry

I think
the water was only looking
for any way out

Two drops on
my sleeve
for a heart or a
bucket

Put away
your
silly
stick

Not so divine

I already know
where the water is

But

I will not
float, swim, or drown
in this flood

until I know
the source

Bricks in a Wall

Helen Patrice

London soft brick:
I'm a small girl squinting my eyes,
guessing at unspoken rules,
cementing in anything that might help.

Lakhori brick:
I'm a teen, making notes in a journal:
'how my friend Elizabeth gets on with boys';
'this is how Karen laughed at a joke'.
Clues everywhere on how to be a real live girl.

Hollow brick:
I'm twenty, in a ballroom,
sitting beside a man:
does his smile mean interest,
or 'interest'?

Sun-dried brick:
should new mother me
be happy about my baby?
The other mothers in the maternity ward
are glowing,
while I shudder in shock at unexpected lovepain.

Jhama brick:
overburnt, strong,
but I can still be broken
with enough effort.

Fire brick:
another online session with my psychologist,
who asks: 'what do you want to work on today?'
I look down at myself,
an unsteady edifice of mismatched colours,
crumbling and new mortar combined.

A poetry prompt asks me
to write a happy or sad poem,
when I know smiles lie,
tears can be for joy,
and my own feelings are
unlabelled bricks.

The Shadows Dance Upon the Wall
(Cento)

Rosemary Nissen-Wade

And that recurrent dream of years ago, pulling
lilacs out of the dead lands, mixing
peculiar unthinkable happenstances ...

I can't understand, no I can't understand.
None of it really happening –
don't tell me it will be alright.

We trip on melted sidewalks,
boots pounding cobblestones,
until we reach that horizon

& in a moment it came back to me, that scent of wet
when I started having tender thoughts about
being eaten by the earth –

to be the stone that splits the stream of their vision
with secret inward gleams
in a radiance dimly akin to happiness.

Consumed, consuming, we are consumed.
The ocean has lost her baby teeth.
I hear it in the deep heart's core –

a heart inflamed ...
altered, estranged, disintegrated, lost.
I wish I was heartless to the core!

But only so an hour,
and then my heart with pleasure fills.
There's so much I want to tell you ...

When only the moon rages,
light lingering in the sky,
night turns dark and gold;

through the dark robe oft amber rays prevail.
My life held precariously in the seeing,
it did not matter if I believed.

(Author's note: A cento consists of lines taken from other poems. It's obligatory to credit the poets used. See the next page for my list.)

SOURCES:

Title:
Samuel Taylor Coleridge

Verses:
J.D. McClatchy
T.S. Eliot
Asha Dutton

Skeeter Davis
Brenda Shaughnessy
Leila Mottley

KB Brookins
Sandra Cisneros
Michael Ondaatje
David St. John
Sharon Olds
Tayi Tibble

Gregory Pardlo
Nam Le
Anthony Hecht

Jenny Justice
Amy Ludwig VanDerwater
W.B. Yeats

Kahlil Gibran
Edna St. Vincent Millay
John Chizoba Vincent

Robert Frost
William Wordsworth
Michael Dickman

Dylan Thomas
Charles Simic
Federico Garcia Lorca

John Keats
Frank O'Hara
Jane Hirshfield

As a Caregiver, I Learn to Lie Better

Delaina J. Miller

He asks to go home,
the cocoon of four walls,
a picture gallery, a tapestry
of a half-remembered life.

        sticky strings
            tiny fibs
        webbing spun

Bread pudding and pears
are welcome distractions.
Longings and loneliness,
hungers harder to satisfy.

        threads of truth
           twist and turn
        knotted yarns

Latticework of fabrications
patch the missing pieces:
car keys, wallet, wife—
freedom and other plunders.

        gossamer
                out of grace
           glistening

Each deception, each ruse,
a selfless caregiver's toll,
the price of compassion
that rends my wretched soul.

Eclipse

Leigh D.C. Spencer

There was an eclipse
today

I got to see it
because my son had
some of those
special glasses

They remind me
of the 3-D viewers
you used to get at
movie theaters

Cheap paper frames and
colored cellophane panels

back when the technology
was new

It's older now
and better

Like me

Well
older anyway

My son warned me
the glasses would
make my world dark

So I shouldn't put them on
before I was settled and
not walking anywhere

I obeyed

I stared
at a sun gone dark

Sliver of light remaining

Darkness
just passing through

long enough to make wiggly
crescent shadow puppets
before the light returned

A beautiful world
where passing darkness
can be calculated

And we are one
in the wonder
of it all

It isn't always so

Our eclipse ended around noon

I walked back to the house
in my own
remaining darkness

and made lunch

The Sad Anniversaries
(Persephone in the Overwolrd)

Rosemary Nissen-Wade

They are now at the further
end of the year, those months
when I return to you – months,
others imagine, of darkness.

They don't know how, when I'm
here in the everyday, I might
yearn for those ghostly passages,
to connect back deeply to you:

You – who dwell, truly, in the realm
of the dead. So I must come to you,
revisiting that now familiar underworld
where those whom we have buried live.

The deep months, when I seem to
withdraw, to disappear, when I am indeed
communing with shadows – they are the
sad anniversaries, the times of ending.

I have adjusted to going back and forth
each year. I do rejoice in the good green
earth, in flowers and the sun. I do
value my living loves, always. And

I watch as they gradually join you
in the tombs of mind and memory …
New friends arrive. Children and other
young things continue appearing yearly.

It is not unpleasant being here, even
in your absence. Nor is it at all unwelcome
when time spins around again to allow me
to linger once more in your reality, Love.

Comet

Helen Patrice

Oh, poor Pluto,
and other trans-Neptunian objects
out there on the edge,
but I go even further
into the cold night,
and return with greetings from the Oort Cloud.

I pass through the orbit of others,
pulled by their importance,
but never succumbing
to their gravity, their weight.
I'm a light in their skies,
a wonder who portends
famine, end of times, a rain of diamonds.

I take a long ellipse,
travel from Mercury, past Mars,
all the way out to Charon.
Only I know if Persephone truly exists
as more than theoretical numbers.
I am a wandering star,
not at home anywhere,
and certainly not wanting to be the hot centre
of attention.

Smoggy Day/Starry Night

Leigh D.C. Spencer

The city is ugly

I know

There is architecture
art and theatre
fine dining and fashion

But there is also the reek

Garbage in the streets
beggars and thieves
violence, decay, and

big fucking rats
that cats in cosmopolitan collars
would never deign to chase

The city
with its never-ending throngs
of the hurrying, bustling, and impatient
has always made me nervous

But it holds treasures
found nowhere else
and there can be safety
in numbers

Thirty-two kids in my classroom
plus one teacher
and two chaperones
to be precise

They unleashed us
on this overcast day
moist, unpleasant air
trapping scents of
pollution and hot dog cart water
to our refuge—
The Museum of Modern Art

We had four hours
to use our assignment sheet
like a scavenger hunt
making sure we New Jersey-ites
absorbed as much culture
as possible

Four hours
Before meeting on the front steps
buying (the world's best)
pretzels and hot dogs
for the bus ride home
to bland suburban safety

Four hours

Which I spent
staring (Star-ing?) at
The Starry Night

Actually

It was slightly longer than
four hours

Because time ceased to exist
(where is Dali when you need his melting clocks?)

I missed the rendezvous

My nervous teacher
grateful
my obsession was
close to the entrance

I was crying when she found me

Four hours' worth of tears
drying on my face

It wasn't just that it was
Beautiful
(but, oh, it was that!)

My eyes absorbed it all
as messenger

For my skin
that felt the humidity
moisture swirling off the landscape
in a hot, slow-moving breeze

A smell in the air
like rain approaching
or recently passed

Or cypress trees

Or last night's stew
lingering into this morning's bread

My brain
knowing it wasn't real

This village

This world

But the hands!

They were real

They held the brush
decided the hue and thickness
to create movement

To create
a living scene
a heaving breath
from nothingness or
from somewhere darker and
even more bleak

What is most important
for the eyes
for the heart
to see?

The artist

standing back
not much further
than where I am now

Just in another time

Did he see the imperfections?

While I am perfectly
immersed in his canvas
content to never leave?

Canvas

Stretched tight and plied lovingly
with oil-textured dreams
of a living, breathing night
on the edge of a new day
never to be

My brain
can barely grasp

That he
and I
stood
in this same proximity
in this twinkling brilliance

His creation
and my naïve adoration
separated only by
canvas and
time

Time
to go now

With my teacher
who is angry

I didn't follow directions

I can't do the assignment

I am a brat
who still hates the city

Except

for that one afternoon I spent
with Van Gogh

Let's Hear It for Elvis!

Rosemary Nissen-Wade

I was just fifteen
when he burst on the scene.
Could there have been
a more perfect age
for falling in love with Elvis?

The curl of his lip,
the twist of his hip,
the way he let rip –
the whole world a stage
for showcasing beautiful Elvis.

And how he could sing!
Let angelic choirs ring,
they don't do a thing
compared with the King.
The voice of the age
will always and only be Elvis.

Lunch with Lewis Capaldi

Leigh D.C. Spencer

I'd want you to think
I'm one of the cool kids

I haven't wanted anyone
to think that
probably since longer
than you've been alive

We'd be in Glasgow
of course
and I'd be worried
that I was mispronouncing everything
(I swear I will understand every word you say)
sloshing my Cullen Skink
and Irn Bru everywhere
with my shaking hands

Would you think
I'm a disrespectful, tacky American
or just that I'm stupid?

Which is worse?

If I tell you my favorite song
and why
would you start scrolling
on your phone?

Wishing you were on the toilet
instead of in this pub with me
having this forgettable fangirl conversation
for the millionth time?

I could tell you
about the autographed calendar
your face
in concert
in black and white
right next to my work desk

Or the doll of you
on top of my computer screen
that lives in its box on top of
the box that holds Ed Sheeran
(I switch their positions from time to time
depending on who is my favorite that week)

Would it be edgy and honest
or unnecessarily cruel
to tell you
the only song of yours
I don't like
is the one you wrote together?

I still bought the single
for your photos on the case
but I skip it whenever it plays
(I really wanted to love it)

Would you be amused to know
I have a life-size
cardboard cutout of you
that I hid in the shower
to scare my husband?

And a smaller version on my desk,
propped up by a canister of
"CALM THE FUCK DOWN"
Snarky Tea?

Or would you back away slowly,
planning a sternly worded text
to your publicist?

Or maybe you'd be sweet
because I remind you
of your mum

And knowing my thoughts about you
are anything but maternal
I will hope for a tablecloth
to die under

We can't share pizza, Buckfast, and dirty jokes
like old friends

There's too much history
inside my head

I'd prefer an autograph to a
restraining order

I'll stay a nameless face in the stands
screaming my heart out to each lyric

Same dozen songs
on endless repeat
in my car

I desperately hope
that I will get to see and hear you again
as soon as your healing body and mind allow

Would it kill you
to give your fans an update
even when you have nothing to sell?

Maybe I would remind you of your mum

Maybe it's better this way—
to remain an anonymous adorer
in good standing

Never to be known or remembered
as that auld wee daft American
that had lunch with Lewis Capaldi

I couldn't Fall in Love with Aquaman

Rosemary Nissen-Wade

I wanted to. I expected to.
But the cinema seats were deep
and soft, and tilted back ... and
there was all this fighting ...
(Battle scenes – even underwater –
I always find incredibly boring.)

It was good to see our Nic,
slim and beautiful as ever
in a role that was 'different' for her,
as Aquaman's mum – great acting
not really required this time,
although she did all right. I figured
she must have wanted a job
that would bring her home
a while to see her birth family.
And they shot it just up here
at Hastings Point, in the heart
of our subtropics. She'd have known
how beautiful, with what great weather.

Even if Nicole couldn't keep me awake –
and I'm a fan – you'd think Jason Momoa
would've had me glued to the screen.
But no, off I nodded. Afterwards I decided
it wasn't a problem of the heart; just that
it was never Aquaman I lusted for – nor even
cheerful, good-natured Jason himself.

No, it was always Khal Drogo, from the first
instant he appeared onscreen in my home telly.
I don't even go for large, well-muscled men;
I like 'em lean and hungry, thoughtful,
and able to make me laugh. The Khal
shattered every preconception I'd acquired
in my seven decades of life until that moment,
and furthermore turned me young again. Oh,
he was something else! How I miss him –
but his element was fire, not water.

Steam and Succour

Helen Patrice

If I were my teapot,
I'd be warm on this cold autumn day.
I'd sit cozy, round, chubby even.
A writer's hands wrapped around me:
love, anticipation, kindness perhaps,
because I'm naked –
no woollen wrap for me.
I'd be desired,
longed for,
know I contain the best blend
of spice and sweetness.

If I were my chai,
I'd have lovers:
honey and milk,
and they'd await me.
I'd pour out; they'd enter me.
We would swirl, circle,
become one.
I would be consumed, drunk down,
and I'd heat a good body through.

Longing

Rosemary Nissen-Wade

I'm haunted now by longing, as I age –
the remembered longings of youthful loves –
like an old book, where I turn to a page
back near the beginning, to see if it moves
my spirit now as then. Such treasure troves
of beauty and sorrow I hold within!
Yet why, after so long, do they return
to haunt me? I'd resolved to relegate
all to burial chambers. But they burn,
those old flames, flaring … as the hour grows late.

A Soundtrack of Courtship

Delaina J. Miller

Dooby-Dooby-Wah

A lad in denim,
a girl in pearls,
cruising to the dance.
Music sets their scene.

Beggar to a King

Cranked on chemistry,
they sing duets
and dance the jitterbug
into a wedding song.

It's So Easy to Fall in Love

They agitate the gravel,
souped up attitudes
rockin' dreams
into rolling realities.

Come On, Let's Go

Daddy-O and his strait-laced
"chick" flip the flick,
boogie-woogie around the globe
in their smooth suede shoes.

Someone Watching Over You

She made the sandwiches.
He made the moves,
twirling classical
rock-n-roll before its time.

Not Fade Away

Older now, the couple
bebop into their golden years,
a toe-tapping, life-long
affair in denim and pearls.

The Song, 'Suzanne'

Rosemary Nissen-Wade

Because I'd never heard it before, though you knew it at once.
Because we were sitting together in a dimly lit café in Sanur.
Because it was clandestine, and longed-for, and finally happening.
Because the air was warm and fragrant, and the place empty but for us
(because it was back in the seventies, the tourist boom only beginning).
Because it was Neil Diamond singing, and his voice was golden.
Because later you gave me Leonard Cohen's poems and his two novels.
Because the song was so romantic, and being in Bali was so romantic.
Because when we did, our loving in the lamplight was beautiful, magic.
Because you told me in tones of wonder, 'So strange. I'm in love with you,
and I'm not in love with you' and I replied, 'Well, I *hope* you're
in love with me and not in love with me,' and you said fervently, 'I am!'
Because I couldn't find any past-life karma between us, which meant
to me you were simply a gift from Heaven, out of the sheer blue sky.
Because although we couldn't be forever, I could fault you for nothing.
Because you went on to be happy, and I went on to be richly fulfilled.
Because when I wrote my most famous erotic poem I was craving you.
Because of that deserted beach we walked, meeting two naked hippies.
Because the smoke from your joint made curlicues up the walls.
Because you loved literature and music and art and trees and the sea.
And because it's a truly, uniquely, brilliantly evocative song, let's face it.
For all these reasons and more, the song 'Suzanne' still turns me inside-out.

His Blue-Eyed Gal

Delaina J. Miller

I sit with him at his new home,
the one he doesn't share with her—
      his blue-eyed gal.

My eyes are brown.

His teeth worry his bottom lip,
      thoughts flitting,
        unformed on his tongue.

I rest my hand on his shoulder,
a clue of our connection,
      and gradually he returns.

The room brighter now
      with his laughter,

he turns to say something
      already flown, forgotten.

    Yet, he remembers
his wife's blue eyes,
asks the color of his own.

Hazel dims to gray.
        He longs
for the familiar: the sky, the sun.

"She'll visit tomorrow," I tell him.

With a nod,
he slips into his own reality
where she's still beside him.

He doesn't know, but we both mourn
        —the way they were together,
        the way they used to be—
him and his blue-eyed gal.

Torment
('Wuthering Heights' remembered)

Rosemary Nissen-Wade

Little rich girl
forbidden passion
wild-hearted orphan boy
the savage moors.

Respectable marriage
dull but wealthy
life inside walls.

Lover
married for revenge
hating his wife.
Surly. Tyrannical.

How did Cathy die?
How do I not
remember?

The story begins and ends
with her ghost,
crying through the window
to be let in.

Unheard
by the man who lost her –
for all his fierce desire.

Alone, sobbing,
begging her wandering spirit,
please come in
come back to him.

(I understand
that longing
for one dead.)

Sustainable

Leigh D.C. Spencer

It's not like you think
it's going to be

It never is
and you really should
know that by now

Rushing in
tits first
ass over tea kettle
bubbling over
all enthusiasm
no one else matches

So you're left with
a chip here
a chip there

Pieces of yourself
scattered
waiting on a spark
even a damn FLINT
to make a difference

But there's the rub—
you have to build
the fire
Centralized
that teepee triangle
they teach you
in Girl Scouts

Survival
and cookies
and you,

scattering precious kindling
unfocused
to the winds

Waiting on
what?

Community
to bring them back
together

To remember
we all need
the light
and the heat

and I
don't know how
to build a fire
by myself
for myself

So darkness,
then

It's okay

I built that

Centralized
focused
by and for
myself
no flint to spark

Is it weird that
I'm still not cold?

It's never like you think
It's going to be

I really should know that
by now

On Being Asked to Tell a Tall Tale and Make it Funny

Rosemary Nissen-Wade

But I don't feel like laughing, and I've no tales to tell
tall enough to top the reality of our world right now.

Once upon a time a species on this planet grew too fast,
too large. Dinosaurs? No, us: breeding and breeding.

You've seen it with other animals. Overcrowding
leads to aggression, fights to the death.

Sometimes Earth creates plague, or famine, to interrupt
burgeoning numbers. Sometimes that's not enough.

This species became so big it blotted out the sun. Or
perhaps it was the opposite? Anyway, climate changed.

A sudden plague wiped out millions ...
still didn't quite do the job. New wars began –

though most of us knew this was not the way home
to a safe place, living in balance with nature.

What price revolution, if it uses
the same old weapons? Yet –

what price change, if gentle means slow?
We fight for breath. The trap closes.

Man vs Bear

Helen Patrice

It's the debate,
this week,
for a woman to choose a bear over a man
when rambling in the woods.

A bear will show annoyance,
attack, kill, and eat me.
He won't insist I eat him
until he comes,
or he'll attack and kill me.

Goldilocks chose three bears,
and came out
none the worse for a meal,
a sit down,
and a sleep.

I've had men demand sex
for the price of a six-dollar meal,
the privilege of sitting in their car,
and for being left alone long enough
to have a sleep.

Lucky Rose Red
found a prince under a bear's fur.

While I sat in Fish Creek Park,
something brown crashed through undergrowth
on the far side of the river.
Later, I felt something watching me from behind a tree,
heard a soft snuffle
that moved away on clawed, bear feet.

Both times I was less afraid
than when I heard a jogger
coming towards me
his Lynx deodorant giving him away.

Setting the Bar

Leigh D.C. Spencer

He said
"It's the least I can do"

and he did

so I left

The New Proust Questionnaire

Helen Patrice

1. If not yourself, who would you like to be?
2. What is your present state of mind?
3. Have you ever fired a gun?
4. Who is your favourite tyrant?
5. Name the country you'd most like to invade.
6. Is there a monster you'd shoot in the ear?
7. Would you wear a commemorative maxi pad stained with nail polish after the event?
8. How would you occupy yourself in prison?
9. How many compliments can you take in a day?
10. Would you accept fan mail under any circumstances?
11. As a convicted criminal, would you run for president?
12. How do you live with yourself?
13. Does having a gold toilet help?

Conflict

Rosemary Nissen-Wade

Two you'd think should be allies –
who need to live together
in mutual support, symbiosis,
in give and take, ebb and flow,
in response, adaptation
… in balance.

Earth silting over,
piling up, drying out, being shovelled,
rearranged by hands and machines,
becoming inhospitable to water;
Earth discharging its garbage –
being made to discharge its garbage –
to crowd water, to infect water.

Water overflowing –
overflowing the sky in enormous rains;
overflowing the seabed, which
no longer contains it; overflowing
rivers and streams, roaring
to crash over fields, against bridges,
through houses, to inundate and alter
the lives of all who live on the earth.

A conflict deadly for us
who need both earth and water.

Poetic Devices Take a Stand

Helen Patrice

I'm going by Al now,
said Alliteration.
Always, all the time,
Al-literating for all.

I'll be Con,
said Consonance.
I'll stand for romance,
bromance, dance on the tongues
of fancy-pants.

I'm Milly,
said Simile.
Simple like a simian line
right across the palm.

Taffy,
said Metaphor.
Sticky on the tongue.
Taffy, toffee, fudge, caramel.

I'm not playing,
said Assonance.
Just call me Fred.

Tell-Tale Cliches for Caregivers

Delaina J. Miller

You tell me:

>Truth is stranger than fiction,
>that no man is an island,
>anything goes.

You tell me:

>You will protect me from the storm,
>through thick and thin,
>time and time again.

You tell me:

>To look on the bright side,
>every cloud has a silver lining,
>your bags are packed and ready to go.

Things aren't what they used to be:

>I feel your frustration,
>your sadness,
>your grief.

Tell me.

    Tell me.

        Tell me, I matter to you.

Stims

Helen Patrice

I suppose I had my stims smacked out of me.
Any tics, spasms, or habits
received a slap, a rebuke,
an order to stand in the corner of the kitchen,
the classroom.

I turned them inwards.
No one thinks twice if a girl bites her nails.
If I went on to peel down the skin
to expose a soft tender layer
that was painpleasure to rub against my skirt,
that was my small business.

I chewed the inside of my mouth
to nubbins of mince,
then tore away strips of flesh
in runnels that were utter delight
to feel coming away.

Immediate thrill,
then the long days of healing,
so I could do it all over again.
No amount of bad-tasting nail polish
or chewing gum stopped me,
to my mother's horror.

She grabbed at my hands,
pulled down my lip,
said none of this was nice.

At least those stims were subtle.

My beautiful inner world
where I was as sensitive as a snail's antennae,
where I could be naked down past my skin.

The Middle of Me

Delaina J. Miller

At a horizon, the sun blazes
across the ocean, drapes
over mountains and plains.

From another, the moon chases
shadows into crevasses, turns
tall trees to silhouettes.

I stand at the center of everything—
a point of in-between,
a held breath caught in light.

I'm a response to the experience:
      an idea, a life,
         peace, conflict.

Yet, I'm also a riddle unsolved,
a ripple as it stretches
toward a mystery shore:

      a simple reverb
      of birth on a journey
      to the final breath.

The Promise That Never Came True

Rosemary Nissen-Wade

'Don't pull faces',
the grown-ups always said.
'If the wind changes,
your face will stay like that'.

It wasn't true.
We tried so hard, but never
could fix our faces
in those wonderful distortions.

It didn't occur to us
that maybe our collective parents
hadn't lied. Maybe
we just never caught a wind change.

MELT

Helen Patrice

The open fire in our living room
had a nest of brown coal beside it,
brickettes of smut and shine.
I never saw my mother shovel or haul.
It must have happened while I played
or slept through another cough syrup afternoon.

I sat in front of it on Sunday nights,
allowed a glimpse of *Dr Who*
after the news and endless horse racing results.
She combed my hair slowly,
with a delicious scrape scratch
across my thin scalp
that made me prickle in a way the heat didn't.

I yearned to touch the coal
with my newly washed hand
but was slapped away.
The briquettes shone as though already heating,
just the way hair combing softened and dissolved me.

I saw my pacifier melting in the fire one night –
pink plastic congealing around the flattened rubber.
I was 'Too Big', 'Too Old' to have it,
my mother said.

She ran the comb through my hair,
and it didn't feel quite as good.
Something in me annealed hard,
as I felt my first push of anger
at a decision made for me.

That was the night
my hair became 'difficult'
and did not lie smooth anymore.

Some Days/Other Days

Leigh D.C. Spencer

Some Days

Your hair is wild
as your attention span
and equally
all over the place

But oh, it shines
old pennies and
more nickels
these days

Your eyes shine
wonder of a child
mischief of a woman

Both excited
for the stories
they get to tell

Your face lined
by every laugh
Roared
by every kiss
Puckered
by every worry

Overthought
for those you love

You love
so easily

Old dogs

New friends

Open heart

Rolled up sleeves

making the world
a bit kinder
one drop in the bucket
at a time

I'm proud
of this face in the mirror
of this life lived

I'm excited
for the next adventures

I'm satisfied
with this legacy I leave

when all I am is
a memory

So many stories
funny, warm, and
Weird

Beautiful
as I saw myself
some days

Other Days

It's crazy
for a woman your age
to have hair as long as this

But let it hang
to cover
rheumy and swollen
allergy eyes
and that double chin
like your neck is trying to
swallow your head

Graceless
lurching behemoth
telling stupid jokes

As if anyone cares
what you have to say

SHUT UP!

If you can't be small
be quiet

Do for others
like it or not

You can't remind them
you have any worth
at all
if you say no

If you show up
empty-handed
they will stop
inviting you

You're only as good
as the platter in your hand
so make it GOOD
Don't be pathetic

Don't cry

Don't ask for help

Maybe just…

Don't
get out of bed
at all
these days

A Metaphor of Donuts

Delaina J. Miller

Divine and sweet,
sugary glaze—
      Oh, such a treat!
— doughy circles,
deep fried in heat.

Body and soul greet
the cycle of life—
      breath and heartbeat!
—oneness in the whole
rounded to repeat.

Fillings of great feat,
brie and lavender—
      Yeah, it's unique!
—but there are those of us,
that like mincemeat

and things bittersweet.
Slowly we warm—
      even feel complete!
—to the recipe
of our self-deceit.

Beat Figuratively, Mostly

Helen Patrice

Take one small girl mixed
into a neurotypical society.
Beat – figuratively.
Let sit.

Tell her it's normal to love the world.

Allow to rise
in a warm country,
in a middle-class home
where it was 'boy children only'
until she was born.

Add one mildly (neuro)spiced boyfriend,
lukewarm,
straight from his mother's apron strings.
Let the girl think she's found a home.

Tell her it's normal and good and grown up to fall hard for her first.

Fold and roll, and fold again.
Prove in an uninsulated house
in an isolated suburb.
Stud with chocolate bullying
and cardamom pod opinions.

Tell her that we don't talk about abuse:
it's not nice.

Add two children
one with autism, intellectual impairment,
and non-speech.
The other with hearing aids,
and an aching need to be just like the other girls.
It gives a good spice flavour.

Tell her she must just gushlove being a mother.

Add eggs, hard-boiled
just as the girl/woman becomes.
Mix until she's dizzy.
Extract as much of the husband as you can.
Use a cold spoon.

Bake in a sole-parent warm oven.
Do not check.

Tell her she's strong while she's crying.

Cool on a rack,
the one with ropes and cogs.

When cold, slice into servings.
This much for one child,
that much for the other,
one portion for work,
one for government accountability,
one for the bank.
Keep cutting away,
up, through.

Tell the woman selfhood will have to wait,
because people depend on her.
Layer on with multiple breakdowns

that she masks away behind a rictus smile.
Serve in pieces on fancy plates.
If she doesn't look like the picture in the book,
that's okay.

Tell her to love herself,
the world, humanity.

In Media Res

Leigh D.C. Spencer

I have no idea
when I'm going to die

Thankfully

Because if I have to
calendar one more fucking thing
my head just might explode
in a rush of gore and
self-fulfilling prophecy

So I don't know
which of my chapters is
mid-life

I'm not dramatic enough
to even call this a crisis

But
at the (over)ripe age
of fifty-three
I jumped my story back
to the middle

Back
to that time
when I was twenty-two
and I was so sure
I wanted to be
a teacher

We all dream
about younger days
things (and people)
we'd do differently
if we had the chance

But when you realize
outside the dream
that your current path
is suffocating you
in bullshit
not remotely worth
dying for

You create new chances

You choose
an alternate variation
on your (one and only) adventure

Turn left this time
instead of right

See what happens

Even when
the years ahead are very likely
fewer
than those behind

Next week
I celebrate
my first day of school

For the first time
in thirty years

I'm looking forward
to 17th grade

I'm looking forward

Because
I'd rather be swimming
even only halfway to my goal

Than drown
treading water
where I was

Return Me

Delaina J. Miller

When my body heaves its last
      murmur, cleanse me in fire.

Take my ashes to the roots
      of wild oaks, my ancestors.

Scatter me with the aspens'
      cheerful jazz-hand leaves.

Render my peaceful soul
      to the symphony of trees.

Not All Is Lost

Delaina J. Miller

Notice the delicacy
    of wings,

notice the luxury
    of a sunrise,

notice the resilience
    of waves,

        even as each solar lap
            brings an end.

Notice the might
    of butterflies,

notice the seasons
    of the earth,

notice the flexibility
    of lava,

        even as each solar lap
            brings an end.

Dreams rise
      in the open sky.

A rainbow arches
      in sunbathed rain.

Among the simple and the fierce,
      we exist.

            Not all is lost,
            even as each solar lap
                  brings an end.

Figs

Leigh D.C. Spencer

I've always wanted
a fig tree

I adore the fruit

But also the
look and feel
of leaves like
leathery medieval
mittens

I imagine myself
a fairy
beneath the mossy shady bowers

Mythical creatures resembling
friendly rats
nibble the dried sweet fruits
fallen early

While I wait
for the purple bursting
ripeness

Perfection
to reality

My tree
my sapling fig
survived the winter

Joy and relief as I tower over
new leaves

I hope
for more winters
and springs

Just like this

I can almost taste
my figs

Observing Poppi

Rosemary Nissen-Wade

I watch how her fur catches the sun.
It's not really black. The highlights gleam
a warm reddish-brown.
I watch her curl and flex and stretch,
doing her slow cat-yoga routine,
then I reach to stroke her soft belly.
She folds herself in,
purrs, relaxes … and shifts into dream.
Where do our souls wander, after the light is gone?

As I Move Nearer

Rosemary Nissen-Wade

As I move nearer to death, memory gathers the scraps of my life.

The Living Treasures of Memories

Delaina J. Miller

    What does it mean to live
    after
           the mind slips into itself?

    A treasure chest
        of memories
                of a life

        hidden,
and the map
    self-destructing.

I watch his reclined body;
his chest rises and falls,
as breath comes and goes.

His eyes move beneath
eyelids as if they are
watching something.
His hand rises, reaching—
he grabs at the air
and stretches further.

             There's only
    the vision
                    and the void.
    The quest
            offers
    one player   at a time.

             The hero
    alone
                 journeys.

The diagnosis means:
the familiar becomes forgotten,
memories turn to vapory wisps.

Our shared treasures
no longer safe in our arms,
we hold them in our chests.

Our united experience
a map
of different paths.

        The living transits
        to legend
                behind closed lids.

        Lost in himself;
                this is what it means
        to venture within.

        The seeker sees
                horizons change,
        trails grow cold.

The hole where he rests
too shallow to hold
the value of his life.

In grief's wake, I'm left
with swollen, wet eyes
and my heavy, full heart.

I know the treasures
of life, bounties
brimming with love.

A Surreal Day
(Letting Go of Julian)

Rosemary Nissen-Wade

1.
The thorn in my eye makes it weep, not bleed. I cover it with
my hand, to watch, one-eyed, a gigantic white-haired man who
ages years as I look. When I can see again two-eyed – the barb
withdrawn from an eye dimmed but not entirely wrecked – it is to
observe glass flowers shatter in front of me, suddenly. I forget the
man who loomed so large; forget how, daily, hourly, he is shrinking
even as I fail to watch.

2.
What is the nature of reality?
As my friend drives us to another town
for *The Trust Fall* movie that we missed here,
the pollen-heavy miles inflame my eyes.
In a strange, surreal state, I watch the screen
with a hand covering each eye in turn
(to cut glare, soothe pain) as we all observe
a far less transient torture, long-term,
likely to be fatal. It's clear the man
is not villain but hero. How can we
save him? It needs all of us to keep on!
Home, I manage to smash a favourite
glass. Upset, I forget Assange – once more
blanking out that we live in the unreal.

(Author's note: This was written before Julian Assange was released from Belmarsh prison.)

HERO

Helen Patrice

Super: Star, Success, Man, Woman,
Girl, Dog, Mother—
all the Supers saving the world,
inspiring, doing what's right.

I don't like Super stories:
an athlete, actor, writer,
coming out of nowhere (supposedly),
dazzling the world with Incredible feats
of strength, endurance,
piercing insight into the heart of mundane America.
Some Armstrong, Oprah, or Rowling
cruising the skies above Metropolis.

I love Black Widow,
who trained hard,
got good at her game.
No tech, no magic hammer,
no green anger hulking her bigger.
Just her, in skin-tight leather,
using everything she's learned
over long, cold Siberian years.
Karate-kicking naysayers
and mansplainers into adamantian jails,
then getting a fresh coat of polish
on her nails.

I invoke her when the work is tough,
when some government official
thinks he has been radiation-enhanced,
and wants to say that my son
Autism Man,
is less than human,
less than Super.

The Dream Maker

Delaina J. Miller

A man of the heart
      hears
      helps
offers his outstretched
      hand.

A man of action
      listens
      plans
his heart in his outstretched
      hand.

A man of the heart
      inspires
      sustains
your success his award:
      "Thank you, ma'am."

Measured by beats,
      together
      you stand,
hand over heart,
      he owns the brand.

Mysterious Underworld
(What If Our Whole Worldview Is a Mistake?)

Rosemary Nissen-Wade

I learned today of the invisible underground jungle:
millions of microscopic animals and plants,
competing with each other, eating each other,
some helping and some harming the larger earth –
millions in every grain of soil – and evidence of others
too tiny to yet be discerned. Scientists now (of course!)
are plotting how to harness them into humanity's service.

How much do these infinitesimal creatures perceive
of our reality? If we can't see them, can they see us?
Surely we must be too huge to them to be viewable
in our entirety – if at all. Do they get any sense
of some greater agency, barely comprehensible?
Do they have notions of our existence, much like
the way we postulate deities, angels, even demons?

What if there's an infinite progression? What if we,
and all the life forms our bare, unmagnified eyes discern,
and even our vast, swirling galaxies, are in our turn
similarly minute to some other beings whose existence
we fail to glimpse, let alone comprehend? What if
it never stops? If that's the true nature of infinity?
Are we helping or harming a world we can't imagine?

Hercules in the Sauna

Helen Patrice

They move away from him.

    He takes up space.
    Tired muscles unable to relax.
    He's laboured hard,
    needs this time of steam and rest.
    A chance to poach the ache out
    of his arms, back, legs.

Gods' Almighty, the stink!
Overpowering the good man-god sweat
is horse-shit reek
that ten maidens with ten scrubbing brushes
couldn't get out of his pores, his nails.

    He needs to talk –
    to someone, anyone,
    about what he did,
    and how he's paying and paying.
    How no amount of pine resin on the coals
    scalds away the pain.

The others, courtiers of King Eurystheus,
hangers-on greedy as Stymphalian birds,
move away from him.
He's ruining their steam and soak.

They paid good money for this time,
and tomorrow they'll mount their horses
from the Augean stables
(beautifully clean now)
and hunt pheasant,
just for the pleasure of it.

Arguing with the Nature Spirits

Rosemary Nissen-Wade

Hey woman, hooray for you!
You've left us a nice mini-jungle here
within your small back yard.
We do like to be left some suitably
untouched, wild spaces – especially now
when, all around us, foolish folk
allow the wilderness to diminish.
We fear it will all disappear too soon.

I understand that greed for wilderness.
Yet if I allow the weeds to continue
rising unchecked in rich proliferation,
soon I'll have the whole snake nation
sunning there, nesting there, as the weather
warms and draws them out from hibernation.

Oh no, we've seen you do it before:
you'll get that kid from over the road
to come again, to prune and pare,
weed widely, crash through and slash
all the tall stems and grasses,
until at last – wanna bet? –
there'll be nothing much left,
and some of us will be out on our arses.

*It'll be me out if I don't please the landlord
with some attempt at suburban order:
a border here, a mown lawn there, while I grow
sweet European flowers to be weeded, watered,
pruned, and generally mollycoddled. I need
to keep this rented roof over my old head.*

We're looking for good weedy plots with lots
of room, lots of thick growth. Too much neatness
makes us needy! So, OK, you rent; which means
appeasing your landlord's conventional silliness.
But must you till every small corner? Must you
cut and cultivate so fully, so tidily, so prettily,
so politely? Why not leave us just one little bit?
What if we promise to chase away snakes?

The Starry Night Wikipedia Entry

Helen Patrice

In the aftermath of his breakdown,
Vincent painted his night view.

> In the aftermath of my breakdown,
> my nights were studded with small white pills,
> prescribed by a psychiatrist who saw me twice.

The breakdown resulted in the self-mutilation of his left ear.

> The breakdown resulted in homelessness,
> stealing leftovers from cafés.

Housed in a former monastery.

> Refuged in my green Mazda, big enough for sleeping
> hunched.

During this period, he produced some
of his best-known works.

> During this period, my ex kept my clothes,
> money, computer, phone.

He painted the view no fewer than twenty-one times.

> I took 40 milligrams of Valium daily.

The Starry Night is the only nocturne.

    My nights were dreamless.

Venus was visible at dawn in Provence.

    Venus, the Goddess, crying for me,
    and me crying for everything.

Critics stop short of calling it an hallucinatory vision.

    It took months to let go of the dream of jumping off Black
    Rock

    a swirl of bloody colours, and texture
    smashed on the shoal below.

The Rattlesnake
(Inspired by The Rattlesnake sculpture by Frederic Remington)

Delaina J. Miller

    together
we stroll along
  through life
    our eyes
      focus
on the path ahead
  our ears
    tune
to the noise
  in our minds
and we miss
      the rattle
that quakes the ground

Haiku Corner

Leigh D.C. Spencer

Eyes barely open
new daylight and a warm dog
bring the sun to me

Inhale messy life
All this and I am enough
Exhale perfection

Rushing creek, smooth rocks
Only battering and time
calm our rough edges

A Fisherman's Tale

Delaina J. Miller

He rambles about the woods he knows so well.
He goes twice every year. Bitter white winters
for elk. Narrow rapid rivers for trout.
Some look for peace in church. He captures
bliss in the rugged Rocky's aspens and pine.

He wades into a cold stream and flicks his arm
back and forth from his side with all the flair
of skipping stones. His fly—Parachute Adams—
leaves ripples in its wake. Meditative,
he plays catch and release with fish for hours.

With a crack, he turns to see on the bank,
mamma bear, as she stands tall and roars.
Two cubs tumble like river stones
to her side. He pulls back to make his retreat
—just as a trout eagerly snaps up the fly.

As quick as he can, he reels in the line
and throws her his catch; mamma traps the fish
in massive claws. After their meal, the bears waddle
into the trees. The fisherman sighs his praise
that, today, he is the one that got away.

Tell Me a Story

Leigh D.C. Spencer

I started collecting
children's books
long before
I had anyone
to read to

My first baby
had a veritable
library of
dragons and rhymes

Fairytales
traditional and wonderfully
twisted

Unconventional heroes
bats, roaches, narwhals, and snakes
along with
Very Hungry Caterpillars
Morality
Compassion
Sillyness
Curiosity
Security

The power
of words and
imagination

A literary recipe
for a happy childhood
prepared nightly
by my eager
loving voice

Before me
my grandmother
gave life to
Alice and Jabberwocky
Walruses and Carpenters

Dramatic voices in a
Jersey accent
to my rapt wonder
adoring the gift of
each page

I wanted the same
for you
Long days end
cuddled in with
what happens next
and sweet dreams

I hoped
you would recognize
the treasure
of it all

Inheriting
the library
to build and share
in your own voice
to your someday children
to add your link
to the chain

Time will tell

But please know—
you're never too old
for bedtime stories

This full circle
Truth
applies
to us both

When my time
as teller is passing

Please

Tell me all about
dragons and rhymes

Let me bask
in the magic
in the love
in the joy
of each turning page

until the last

Stamps of the World

Rosemary Nissen-Wade

Why does Portugal love Snoopy? Why
do such a lot of other countries love cats?
Silly questions! I love Snoopy and cats.

Mt Fuji makes sense for Japan.
Are flowers / birds / fungi national?
What about lobsters? Bats?

I'm more used to monarchs (British)
notables from history (Australian)
images of public events.

In the middle of my childhood
when I started to be serious,
(before I turned teenage frivolous)

Grandpa decided I'd collect stamps
like him; spent hours sitting with me
to explain their stories, their geography.

I didn't care about small squares of paper.
I wanted books. It was books, not stamps,
brought messages, showed me the world.

Who uses stamps now? We email, we text.
But books continue to bring me mountains,
flowers, animals, cartoon characters …

Rumpelmayer's
(for Tante Tuna)

Leigh D.C. Spencer

It was the fanciest place
I'd ever been

I probably
wasn't dressed for it

But she didn't care

My fancy Aunt
treated me
on my birthday

How old?
I don't remember

Old enough
to sit still-ish
and not break anything

Young enough
to be awestricken

by the pink
and gold walls

Teddy bears
posh and plush
seated at empty chairs

You were allowed
to cuddle them!

While sipping
gourmet hot chocolate
thick and rich

warming you
down to the toes

Manhattan snow
dripping slowly
off your new boots
onto the fancy carpet

It couldn't possibly
get better

Until your Aunt
your partner in crime
gets a twinkle in her eyes

She summons
the dessert cart

It's shining silver
and it looks like
Cinderella's carriage

piled with pastel pastries
like edible ballgowns

Creams and fondants
chocolate in every color

And you
the Birthday Princess
(with skinned tomboy knees
and a bad home haircut)
are somehow
supposed to choose

But your Aunt is
the fancy one
so you defer
to her wisdom

Indeed, a wise choice!

Because she also
can't decide

You watch as
plate after plate
of tiny, sugared perfection
is piled from the cart
to your table

You try (at least)
a bite of them ALL

stuffed
like the crumb-coated
teddy bear in your grip

The bill is paid with a smile

Sugar drunk
you hop down
from the fancy chair

Recognizing
you are leaving
a place of magic
probably never to return

(You will—next year!)

Temporary Princess
a pout to tip your crown
flipped
by another choice

"Any stuffed animal you want!"

from the toy store
at the exit

A white dog
(that I still have!)
named Snowball Kelly
rides on my lap

back home to New Jersey

Wonderous Things, Rainbows

Delaina J. Miller

As a child, I was fascinated
with rainbows, the promise
of the pot of gold.
But which side held the treasure?
Was one person's end
my beginning?
Do the colors narrow
when they touch the ground?
I could spend its lifespan
      in wonder.

As an adult, I find
sacredness in rainbows.
Perspective deepens their intensity,
the beginning, and the end.
They are the reward
for looking up,
the arc of breath while grieving,
the awe of light bending
into life's colorful moments—
      refractions.

Talking with the Dead

Leigh D.C. Spencer

She says there are ways

If I am open

If I quiet the noise
in my over-busy brain

they might come

I suck
at meditation
at all forms of
relaxation, really

I can't cheat
with a Ouija board
because I might open
an uncloseable door

The one I want most
to talk to
couldn't spell anyway

But if there's a way
I'm sure she's here

Shaking her head over
my week night tater tots
my filthy white floors
my sloppy house clothes
my (almost always) bare feet

Still bursting with pride

Over me
Over them

A whole new generation
of our blue eyes and
kind, round faces
that she only barely
got to meet

Tell me

how it is
that I got your
kopitkis recipe
SO WRONG
even the dogs
wouldn't eat it?

Teach me

to do it right
even just
one more time

She talks to the dead
says there are ways

I believe her
I am open
I am trying my best

to be quiet
to let you
talk

A Remix of Gratitude

Delaina J. Miller

What is space? Invisible
      made visible with perception.
Fragile is that moment
      between nothing and everything.
Together, we build a connection
      in the soil of humanity.

Mini-Mum

Helen Patrice

I was the shortest woman
in prenatal class,
lugging around a belly
big as a watermelon,
sporting a husband
who brayed mocking laughter like an ass.

I didn't have room in me to say:
    'Quiet'.
    'Leave'.
    'I don't want this'.

He was Bottom, a fool entranced
by the fairy realm of a nuclear family,
a man who had a list of every possession he ever wanted,
the last three items being:
    House.
    Wife.
    Two kids.

I was young,
thrilled by the Titania-enchantment
of first love, first baby,
first everything.
An innocent incubator, portable womb
to serve, like Peaseblossom,
like Moth to a flame.

I kept my thoughts minimized,
and was thus perfect –
a Manic Pixie Dream Girl
he could conjure into submission,
and stamp out every inch of sparkle.

Stereotypes

Leigh D.C. Spencer

Two Jews walk into a bar

Okay
more like one
and a half Jews

But anyway

The first Jew
says to the other Jew
"Can I buy you a drink?"

Which is weird
because Jews are supposedly
cheap

But this one seems
willing
even excited
to spend some money

Buying a drink
for the handsome man
she came in with

And he
honoring
his (frugal) half
Jewishness
accepts her offer

He's not sure
what he wants

So she
used to taking the lead
orders
for them both

Plastic glasses raised
filled with something
pink and sweet
she boldly toasts

"Happy twenty-first birthday
to my awesome
(half-Jewish)
eldest son!"

L'chaim!

The Mordialloc Fairies—A True Story

Helen Patrice

The two fairy sisters
in faded orange and pink ballgowns,
secondhand silver sequins,
and brand-new blue sparkle and fluff wands
lived in the seaside town,
near the big road roundabout
that grown men were afraid to drive.
Grown up and old there,
never married,
devoted to each other,
and anything that shone.

Their house, an inheritance,
was ramshackle wooden slats on rotting stumps.
Their garage leaned far to the left,
perhaps whispering to the grey paling fence.
Their front yard was a happy jungle of nasturtiums
and mint run wild.
Two neutered black cats, miniature panthers
stalked the undergrowth.
Do the fae have familiars, like witches?

A young mother gasped when the old women
bent over her curious toddler,
who was in awe,
face shining with delight.

'I wanted to give him the gift of beauty',
said the older sister, sad,
as yet again, Officer Bourke was called to the scene,
and escorted the sisters home.

One hot afternoon they barbecued naked
in the floral centre of the roundabout,
offering sausages and spells
to all who slowed down and honked.

After their arrest,
Bourke was heard to remark –
not complain, but muse
that he'd never get the glitter
out of his uniform.

Shades of Purple

Rosemary Nissen-Wade

I didn't wait to be old to wear purple.
I don't need to dress in black to be a witch.
I've worn purple (with touches of black)
just for the love of it, all my adult life.

My magic cloak is rich magenta –
though I know why witches of old
wore hooded cloaks of black, as they crept
at midnight to their woodland rites.

It was dangerous then to be known.
Best to blend into shade, unseen.
It may still be wise, today, to stay discreet –
but now we're disguised by light, by colour.

Even when I shift to dragon shape,
my silver scales have purple undersides
which cast a play of faint mauve shadows,
a ripple of lilac or lavender, if you blink.

But you won't observe me shift. You won't see
my dragon shape at all. You'll never know
I'm a magical being. You'll love me sweetly
in all shades of purple, believing I have no secrets.

A Painted Shock to the Senses

Helen Patrice

The old train seats are muted
from sunshine and use,
and the handholds always have been
a soft green, easy on the eye,
if not the hand.

Melburnians are a Sunday sea of black clothes,
intent on phones, books,
or their own sunglassed thoughts.
They sit within the carriage,
protected from sunglare by tinted windows.

Outside, asphalt stations
and faded gum trees stream past.
The sky has lost its summer brilliance
and is the steady powder of coming winter.
Grey, brown, and beige buildings are the norm.

Graffiti shouts loud and brilliant along grey fences:
    HEY DUDE
    DON'T LOG DAINTREE
    GAZOS FOREVER
Artists worked in darkness, in haste,
unafraid of crimson, orange, and neon yellow.
Their work is the only dazzling thing on the line.

Can You Keep a Secret?

Leigh D.C. Spencer

It was too big
this information
this peek behind
such a beautifully curated wall

When it started to fall
when no one knew
when she needed someone
She desperately asked
"Can you keep a secret?"

Of course
I said yes

She was my friend
I wanted to help

Of course!

But it was horrific
in a way my sheltered life
had never seen

And it was juicy
God help me, but
my jealousy dined on this morsel
of proof—there is no perfect life

So I told
ONE person

Did I even bother to ask
if they could keep a secret?

I trusted them
not to tell

As she trusted me
in all our faulty judgement

We are not friends
anymore
not really

My fault
but both our losses

My mistake
was in the casual lie
When she asked
"Can you keep a secret?"

I should have
recognized her dire tone
acknowledged my big mouth
respected our delicate bond

I should have
said, "No"

Haunted

Helen Patrice

That I was no good
is the chant that follows me
through dark hallways
and sits on my chest at night.

Ghosts of old mistakes
change self-portrait eyes
until they look back at me,
stare down,
disappointed.

In the creaking Boo Radley house
of my mind,
I am a small girl, yet again
getting it wrong
because the right way was communicated
on a Ouija board at midnight,
when I was in bed
straining to sleep correctly.

What haunts me
is an incubus heavy as a black hole,
ready to fuck
confidence out of me.

I no sooner lie down
than it
and one hundred waiting cronies
slide out of a wardrobe,
and touch the secret places in my mind.

Communication Breakdowns and Other Caregiver Pitfalls

Delaina J. Miller

It was a mistake
to tell you too many words
all at once like that:
to speak too fast,
to explain too much.

It was a blunder
to remind you of what was
just said; or to say:
"You just told me that."
"You saw me yesterday."

It was a fumble
to ask if you remember—
something or someone.
Too familiar, the pit
—the slip of the mind.

There are missteps, sure.
You're doing the best you can.
I forgot, myself,
that it's also true,
I'm doing the best I can, too.

Luck Is Not Chance
(Emily Dickinson and Lady Macbeth)

Helen Patrice

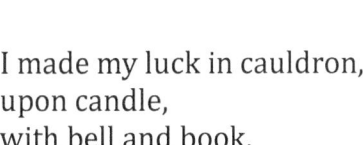

I made my luck in cauldron,
upon candle,
with bell and book,
from power and will.

It was not luck
that had my husband see the witches
on that dark and stormy night.
A blindworm's sting
and a waxing moon
drew him as surely
as wool woven on a spindle.

They positioned themselves well
on his path,
compelled to be there
when otherwise they'd be tucked in their beds.

Luck is what comes from effort.
I was not lucky
to be married to a man
whose ambition was still sleeping.

The quiet of Glamis did not suit me.

My magic and heart
were as strong as an adder's tongue.

Do Better

Leigh D.C. Spencer

The saying goes
"When you know better,
do better"

It's true

But I wish it went
even further

Because we know better
only when we continue
to learn

When we challenge
our precious beliefs
over intervals of time
over experiences of life

Much like
spring cleaning

There's no shame in
wearing a new perspective

when you realize
the world is

so much bigger
than the view
from your bedroom window

There are hills
that I will die on

metaphorically
until my last
literal breath

No question
of right or wrong

No way
I will ever
change my mind

But these are
minor topographies
in the grand scheme map
of everything
I don't know (yet)

For everything else
let me be
a compassionate traveler
a student of the world

an open mind on
an open road

Please
let me know
to do no harm

in my quest
to learn
to do better

Firewalking

Delaina J. Miller

The bed of hot coals sear,
      blister our feet.

The soles of our shoes
      curl like escargot.

Caregivers learn
      to take things in stride.

We move with purpose,
      a test of faith.

It's a journey of soul,
      embers of hope.

Incandescent / Until Burnt Out

Rosemary Nissen-Wade

Can poetry's fire flare out?
If stoked too hard will it blaze
too fierce, soar so high
it thins, becomes air?
Or will it re-ignite?

Your Favorite Quote and the Long Goodbye

Delaina J. Miller

The harder you work:

    From the porch we watch
    the sunset soften—
    glorious to glimmer.

    I look at you expecting
    to see the smile my heart feels,
    but your lips form a flat line.

    Vacancy deepens your eyes;
    you feel far away
    even though I'm holding your hand.

    Memories crash against my ribs,
    and a tide of emotion
    pulls breath from my lungs.

    I mourn how you were
    and wish hard work was enough
    to stretch sunlight and keep you near.

The luckier you get:

> From the porch we watch
> the sky darken—
> scarlet to sapphire.
>
> You suddenly laugh;
> I look at you, and there's
> a grin instead of firm lips.
>
> Twilight sparkles in your eyes,
> and a wave of warm gratitude
> spreads through my body.
>
> The taste of tears will come,
> but in this moment,
> I honor what is, what's now.
>
> The night sky offers an ocean
> of stars to catch our wishes.
> You're right; we are lucky.

Grilled Cheese & Narwhals

Leigh D.C. Spencer

On long days
when I am spent
to the red

feeling small and
awkward and
not enough

I am lucky

for cozy narwhal pajamas
with a hood I can hide under
as long as
I need

for a feisty old dog
who will jump on me
flying fluff and smiles
just checking in
before returning
to the task of dozing
in whichever bed
is closest to me

for my son
who will randomly wander in
to kiss my head
while I'm writing

(Who knows what,
but always something)

and he treats it with
Reverence

like the perfect
grilled cheese
I'll make him
for dinner

because I'm sad today
and it's all I can muster

He looks at the crisped golden bread
corners of melting cheese
like bright orange arrows
advancing on his plate

kisses my head again
through the narwhal hood

He thinks
he's so lucky

I know
we are

Little Lonsdale Street

Helen Patrice

Little Lon runs contrary
to the other one-way streets
in the inner grid of Melbourne.
Lonsdale – an administrator.
Who knows if he would have availed himself
of Little Lonsdale's dirty pleasures?
Brothels, beggars, bullies,
cocaine, con artists, crooks.
No law except the streets.

Now, tall granite buildings
house expensive stores:
the latest and best ways
to part shoppers with money,
as they pin joy
on a bit of skirt,
or a lotion to rub in.
Shop assistants taking money
as johns smile, glass-eyed,
drugged up on hope.

An Atlas of Graditude

Delaina J. Miller

There's value in the area
before the lines intersect,
where neither exist
    together,
and neither exist
    apart.

It's the cartography
of consciousness,
where the Other is
    longitude
a coordinate connection to
    latitude.

Experience forms
the topography of our
landscape. Interaction
    elevates
adding contour and color to
    expansion.

Ley Lines beneath the surface
draw us closer, like a compass
to our true north,
    love
across our life map of
    gratitude.

When and Where Was I Happiest?

Rosemary Nissen-Wade

Let's see. I could say, any and every time
I was near the sea – the magical ocean.
Or when I rose on tiptoe
to sniff deeply of a rose from my father's
beautifully tended bushes.

Or when the moon shone full and bright
through my bedroom window
and I would stay awake
to moon over pen and paper, gazing
out at the night sky and making poems.

It might have been before I was four,
for that was when my dear, kind Nana died.
So much colour and warmth
faded from my life then – the kind
only she could give. That death cost me dear.

All these memories from childhood ...
It's fair, too, to say
that after I fare-welled infancy
to have one of my own,
I thought I'd won the lottery! (I still do.)

His father's blue eyes shone with joy.
(The firstborn's and mine are green-brown hazel.)
I felt so green, so raw, so unprepared –
but I delved into the mine of my own
good memories to unearth what was needed.

When and where was I happiest?
If it's a riddle, I give in.
There's no one answer. Each
of these occasions, and many more,
give me happiness over and over again.

This Is Really Living!

Helen Patrice

He said it as we sat outside
the café full of coffee drinkers.
He fit in
with his black jeans and cappuccino.

    I sat with my pot of chai,
    my separate almond milk and honey,
    stirring until just right,
    wearing a long, loud skirt
    and mismatched jacket made of velvet and lace,
    and all things impractical.

He could pose for hours,
content with his secret thoughts,
looking at nothing.
His plate of toasted tofu and seaweed,
his shot of wheatgrass juice –
his weekly treats.

    I twisted myself like a cinnamon roll,
    drinking the view,
    the people,
    the endless noise,
    the books calling me from stores,
    while I buttered raisin toast
    whose spicy scent blended with the chai,

and both browns suited my red hair
and milk skin.

He lived for Saturdays
of coffee and nothing.

      I craved sugar,
      a bigger life,
      and those books down the road.

Learning To Swear Better

Rosemary Nissen-Wade

'Lonely?' they asked, 'Now
that you're on your own?
Get a pet', they said.
'A faithful dog
or a sweet little kitty'.

But no, I went out
and bought a parrot.
I thought it would be
the ideal companion:
communicative.

I thought I'd teach it
to talk. Ha ha to that!
It must have had
a previous owner. Or,
maybe the pet shop man ...?

No. This bird could only
have belonged to a pirate.
Talk about language!
I could just see him sitting
on Long John Silver's shoulder.

The first time
I dropped something
and uttered a mild 'Damn!'
he went to town,
as if it was a cue.

Astounded by that stream
of colourful invective,
I didn't have a clue
what half of it meant.
But it sounded amazing.

And you can find
anything on Google,
even the worst words.
Next time I listened closely,
looked them up and learned.

Now I'm a pro!
It's fun living alone –
except for my parrot,
who teaches me
all the best words.

Unlikely Chapters

Delaina J. Miller

The Penny Drops

The FBI at the door. A train derailed. Reports of a boy placing something on the track. "Did it smash my penny?" Bobby asks innocently.

Never Proven

Another knock at the door. He was truant—again. The mascot is missing. Bobby's mother gasps. "Yes, that's right," says the school representative. "The cougar is missing. Where's Bobby?"

How to Deal with a Bothersome Brother

Roll him up in a rug at the top of a hill. Matches are optional. But the sight of the flying carpet is more spectacular when lit.

Oh, That Guy!

Bobby tells the person on the phone that it isn't his fault. "My buddy, Ed Westfall, left the rental car on the side of the road." Another explanation: "What? Everyone needs a fall guy."

Venomous Rolly-Pollies

"Watch out for Hoop Snakes!" Bobby warns. "They bite their own tail, so they can chase you faster rolling down the hill." When questioned, he maintains his serious expression. Good thing there's Google.

There's Always an Exception

He's smart as a tack, unless there is a fishing fly caught in a tree. Then it's completely logical to climb said tree. He falls, returns home with two requests: "Take me to the ER" and, the standard, "Don't tell your mom."

Not Going Down for This

His gray hair (what's left of it!) circles his head like an unlikely halo. A cop car pulls near the golf cart. Bobby whispers to his co-pilot, "If we get pulled over, I'm out of here. I've got my good shoes on."

Not Too Late

Delaina J. Miller

Is it really such a tragedy
that my sentence is a structure of
similarity?

> There are still phrases,
> the distinct narratives
> and expressions of me.

Is it really such a disparity
that I wander from room to room
aimlessly?

> There is still recall,
> the places we share,
> keepsakes of you and me.

Is it really such a travesty
that I have forgotten the melody
of your name?

> There is still clarity,
> the feelings of family
> and passion's intensity.

Is it really such an indignity
that the familiar is closer to
novelty?

> There is still joy,
> waltzes to dance
> and serenades to sing.

Is it really such an agony
that I resemble less than
who I used to be?

> There is still my legacy.
> Stop writing my eulogy.
> Let's create a memory
>   before it's too late.

Hex Value #ece63d
(Legal Pad Yellow)

Helen Patrice

At my brother's funeral
Greg sat quiet, but his eyes leapt:
casket, flowers, chapel,
celebrant, funeral director, pallbearers.
His mind was spinning
with the cost of each one.

He was the youngest of three boys –
sons of Hilda,
who kept ledgers for each one –
every single penny she spent.

> Steven:
> baby formula – three dollars,
> doctor visits – fifteen dollars each time.
>
> Alan:
> pacifiers – three pence each,
> five per year, three years.
>
> Greg:
> orthodontia – two hundred pounds.

Food, school fees, ice creams –
everything listed in piles of yellow legal pads
she bought from the newsagent
during the Christmas sales.

At each boy's twenty-first birthday,
she presented them with their totals,
expected a good return on her investments.
And could not stop talking about how each boy
threw his pile, his worth into a bin,
and laughed in her face.
Her outrage, her humiliation, her disgust –
they added up to a stroke at sixty.

Greg at my brother's funeral
quietly asking the chapel director:
How much? Payment plans?
Do the sandwiches cost extra?

Greg caught himself
in the tangle of higher mathematics,
and suddenly subtracted his mother
from himself,
stopping mid-sentence.

He accepted the dusky yellow rose
from my brother's coffin.
There were enough for everyone.
They were the colour of legal pads,
now five dollars a shot
at the newsagent,
even during the Christmas sales.
He threw it in a bin
on his way out.

Security

Delaina J. Miller

I'm small, but
I keep an eye
on your loved one.

Because of me
    you can see
        if they are eating.

Because of me
    you can observe
        how they walk.

Because of me
    you can check
        if they're asleep.

Because of me
    you can hear
        their cries for help.

Because of me
    you can record
        how they're treated.

But I will never give
 the security
 you really desire.

Though there's plenty
of storage in the cloud,
there's no Wi-Fi in heaven.

Historic Event

Rosemary Nissen-Wade

Polar bear;
shrinking scrap
of ice.

At Least

Delaina J. Miller

Can you explain?
    My world has gone odd.

Strings sprout from my feet?
    Legs heavy.

Circles push through holes.
    Chest warms.

Silver scoop carries food.
    Hunger passes.

Brush tickles my tongue.
    Teeth clean.

Stranger in the mirror.
    Face smooth.

Can you explain?
    My world has gone odd.

At least I have you
    to make sense of things.

Not My Dog

Leigh D.C. Spencer

You are beautiful
and aloof

You have no care for
where the humans sleep

You have
dog beds, couches
beds and blankets and
you choose only
at your own whim
where to close your eyes

In your hierarchy
of affections
I come last

But I suspect even
your favorite
could be traded
for a small bite of steak

In the mornings
when I have an empty
Kingsize
all to myself

I call you

I have blankets
so many pillows
a fan blowing perfectly

I beckon you

for cuddles, belly rubs, ear scratches
anything you want
to start both our days in
warmth, love, and security

You pretend you can't hear me

Later
when my mind is immersed
in tasks at hand
your big head
bashes into my arm
demanding attention

I have no choice
but to stop typing, focus
on the noble, immediate purpose of
scratching your butt

I swear
you're like a cat

unfortunately belonging to
not a cat person

I adopted you
because my heart was broken
and you didn't try
to eat our little old dog

It's just that I missed
my dog
so much

I still do

But you

take treats gently
never even think of biting
your people

have unconditional love
for peanut butter
knock over the couch
with your zoomies
have a shoe fetish
make us laugh daily

Very, very occasionally
you rest your velvety head
on my chest
just so

allow me to hug your warmth
stroke your smooth belly
kiss your speckled
Neapolitan ice cream nose

before moving on
to the next comfy spot
that suits you

You are not my dog
as I am not your person

But in these moments
meted and miraculous
there is still love

and you are still
a very good dog

Why I Like Living

Rosemary Nissen-Wade

... although I think my cat does it better. Still,
as I can't be her, I can at least enjoy her –
that sleek, soft fur, and the long, low purr
she gives me when I stroke her after she's
just awoken, or at any time really. And then,
I like the scent of roses – to stoop to them,
low; breathe them in, deep and slow.
What blessings are our noses! Without those
versatile organs, we'd all be losers.
But as one door closes, another opens:
the seasonal flowers must die down
now, in the slowing of autumn, before
being reborn. Yet I can't be forlorn
when every new cloud thrills me with beauty,
or when the moon shines full, or I grab a mango
and taste my fill.

My friend sends a video of her afternoon,
in her new home, peacefully gazing at rain
through her picture window; in the background
Tony Martin and k.d. lang singing – bringing
her own pleasure over the streets and houses to me,
where I'm alone and now no longer alone. Though
the tone of the day might seem subdued, yet I feel
I could rise and dance a fandango, springing
from my chair to whirl in the air, flinging wide

my hands; or segue to a tango, imagining arms
that I have known, fond arms, holding me, bold
and tender, shouldering a kind share of my cares. And
if all I can do now is call on memory, still how I like
to dream and remember ... Yes, I like my living,
I like my loving: all that I've done, and all that as long
as Fate weaves, I will.

The Silence Death Leaves

Delaina J. Miller

With the time we have:

>I cheer you on
>>to hear your spunk.

>I act ridiculous
>>to hear you laugh.

>I play your favorite song
>>to hear you sing.

>I swing your hand
>>to see you smile.

>I rub your shoulders
>>to ease your mind.

>I kiss the top of your head
>>and whisper, "I love you."

With the time we share:

    I know these moments
        are for me alone,

        comfort for
        when the silence comes.

The Cage

Rosemary Nissen-Wade

As I grow
the cage of time
shrinks. My years
expand, filling it.
More and more
the walls close in.

The only window
obscured by a blind,
my little view
is dim, shadowy,
larger vistas
unknown.

In youth, breathing deep
I spread like the branches
of a cedar, yet
with room to spare –
unaware then
of restraining walls.

Present reality
pierces:
a sword.
Almost
I impale myself ...
but, pausing

I glimpse
from the corner of my eye
a jester playing a flute.
His song hints
that time
might be fluid.

What if the walls
are frail, soft
not fixed – if
stepping through
I find that time
is an ocean?

Pause Death

Delaina J. Miller

sun call
        the mourning doves

moon wake
        the sleeping tides

river churn
        the motionless lakes

wind stir
        the breathless hills

clouds clear
        the graying skies

flowers bloom
        among the frozen dew

heart pretend
        we can hold death
                off again

The Prompts That Started It All

There were two different challenges during the month of April. They were NaPoWriMo and Poem A Day (PAD). Here is the list of prompts from both challenges in case you want to play "Guess the Prompt."

Early Bird Prompt
NaPoWriMo: Choose and write about a word from the following word list: cage, ocean, time, cedar, window, sword, flute.

April 1
NaPoWriMo: Write a poem that recounts the plot or some portion of the plot of a novel that you remember having liked but that you haven't read in a long time.
Poem A Day: Write an optimistic poem.

April 2
NaPoWriMo: Write a platonic love poem.
Poem A Day: Write a happy and/or sad poem.

April 3
NaPoWriMo: Write a surreal prose poem.
Poem A Day: Write a musical act or artist poem.

April 4
NaPoWriMo: Write a poem titled or a concept from "The Strangest Things in the World."
Poem A Day: Write a mistake poem.

April 5
NaPoWriMo: Write a poem about how a pair (or trio) of different things would perceive a blessing or something else.
Poem A Day: Write a "tell (blank)" poem.

April 6
NaPoWriMo: Write a poem rooted in "weird wisdom," akin to a strange tidbit someone told you.
Poem A Day: Write a minimum poem.

April 7
NaPoWriMo: Write a poem titled "Wish You Were Here" that takes inspiration from the idea of a postcard.
Poem A Day: Write a luck poem.

April 8
NaPoWriMo: Write a poem that centers around an encounter or relationship between two people or things that shouldn't have really met for some reason.
Poem A Day: Write a major event poem.

April 9
NaPoWriMo: Write a poem as an ode celebrating an everyday object.
Poem A Day: Write a love and/or anti-love poem.

April 10
NaPoWriMo: Write a poem based on one of the headlines, cartoons, or other tidbits from the website "Yesterday's Print."
Poem A Day: Write a "(blank) better" poem.

April 11
NaPoWriMo: Write a poem that honors the "ones" in the number 11 (like a monostich).
Poem A Day: Write a memory poem.

April 12
NaPoWriMo: Write a poem the plays with the idea of a "tall tale."
Poem A Day: Write a funny poem.

April 13
NaPoWriMo: Write a rhyming poem that's based on ten simple words.
Poem A Day: Write a living poem.

April 14
NaPoWriMo: Write a ten-line poem which begins with the same word.
Poem A Day: Write an ekphrastic poem.

April 15
NaPoWriMo: Write a poem that has to do with postage or stamps.
Poem A Day: Write a middle poem.

April 16
NaPoWriMo: Write a poem detailing a place, and then end the poem with an abstract line.
Poem A Day: Write a form and/or an anti-poetic form poem.

April 17
NaPoWriMo: Write a poem inspired by a piece of music.
Poem A Day: Write a "not (blank)" poem.

April 18
NaPoWriMo: Write a poem as if you were "someone" you desire to be.
Poem A Day: Write a pessimistic poem.

April 19
NaPoWriMo: Write a poem about what haunts you.
Poem A Day: Write an emotion poem.

April 20
NaPoWriMo: Write a poem that recounts a historical event.
Poem A Day: Write a six-word poem using: bear, collar, flair, hear, praise, ramble.

April 21
NaPoWriMo: Write a poem that focuses on one color.
Poem A Day: Write a trope poem.

April 22
NaPoWriMo: Write a poem in which two things have a fight.
Poem A Day: Write an earth poem.

April 23
NaPoWriMo: Write a poem about a superhero.
Poem A Day: Write a "(blank) of the heart" and/or "heart of the (blank) poem.

April 24
NaPoWriMo: Write a poem that begins with a line from another poem and take it in a different direction.
Poem A Day: Write a maximum poem.

April 25
NaPoWriMo: Write a poem based on the "Proust Questionnaire."
Poem A Day: Write a homonym poem.

April 26
NaPoWriMo: Write a poem that involves alliteration, consonance, and assonance.
Poem A Day: Write a persona poem.

April 27
NaPoWriMo: Write an American sonnet.
Poem A Day: Write a remix poem.

April 28
NaPoWriMo: Write a sijo-form poem.
Poem A Day: Write a dead poem.

April 29
NaPoWriMo: Take one word from the list *Merriam-Webster* created from Taylor Swift's lyrics and write a poem using that word as the title of your poem.
Poem A Day: Write an "until (blank) poem."

April 30
NaPoWriMo: Write a poem in which the speaker is identified with (or compared to) a character from myth or legend.
Poem A Day: Write a "the end" and/or "a beginning" poem.

ACKNOWLEDGEMENTS

Delaina J. Miller

Delaina would like to thank the incredibly talented: Helen, Leigh, and Rosemary for sharing their lives through poetry and agreeing to a second anthology together. She is extremely grateful for the skills of Carina Bissett for helping her get to the heart of her poetry. Delaina is grateful for her in-laws and family members for the inspiration to write poetry. And, of course, to her wife, Kristin Hatch, for her unwavering support and allowing Delaina to show her grief through words.

Rosemary Nissen-Wade

Rosemary would like to thank her collaborators, Delaina, Leigh, and Helen, for always being a joy to work (and play) with over the years of our individual and collective friendships, and Delaina in particular for being the instigator, prime mover and hard worker behind this book and its predecessor.

She also thanks Australian poet Jennie Fraine for valuable advice on the selection and preliminary editing of her poems, and Carina Bissett for careful editing of the whole book.

She is grateful, too, to the other participants at Maureen Thorson's Na/GloPoWriMo blog, for their interest in and encouragement of poems shared there – and, for similar reasons, Pearl Ketover Prilik and the members of PA – Poeming Friends on Facebook, a group of poets who met as some of the original responders to the annual April Poem A Day prompts at Poetic Asides.

Helen Patrice

Helen would like to thank Delaina, Leigh, and Rosemary for suggesting this second volume of poetry, and Carina Bissett for help in editing her poems. Thanks must also go to her husband Bill for giving her the space to daydream, swear, and eventually chisel words onto the page. Thanks also to Chloe Ballerina Kitty who made the writing ten times harder. No, I will not be writing an ode to your butt, Chloe.

Leigh D.C. Spencer

Leigh would like to thank her family and friends—especially husband Earl, sons Zac and Henry, and dogs Bailey and Sherlock—for being an endless source of inspiration. Thank you for filling my life and my pages. I hope you like what you see. If not, that's on you for associating with a writer. Make better choices. Neener neener.

Leigh would also like to thank the vibrant and generous writers she associates with, particularly Rosemary, Delaina, Helen, and editor Carina. If not for your faith and tenacity, always making room for me at the table, my poetry would be wasted on my dogs. One is deaf, and one is extremely judgy. Thank you for letting me make beautiful books with you!

Additional Acknowledgements

All of the poets would like to thank Jeanie Tomanek for allowing them to use her art *No Woman Is an Island* on the cover. Thanks also to Allison Pang for her design skills in creating a dynamic cover and interior for *Paper Birds*.

About the Poet: Delaina J. Miller

Delaina Miller is a poet, publisher, sound therapist, Reiki Master, and caregiver. Delaina writes poetry because it's her favorite medium to capture snippets of the human experience. She creates Soundology as an energy health modality because she believes music is the rhythm of our soul. Other poetry books by Delaina include *She Too: Four Voices in (Almost) Harmony* and *The Unique and Sundry*. You can listen to her albums and singles from your favorite streaming platform.

About the Poet: Rosemary Nissen-Wade

Poet, memoirist. Author of several monographs and chapbooks; included in various collaborative works (such as this) and numerous magazines and anthologies over the years.

Performance poet, reviewer, editor, poetry blogger, facilitator of writers' groups on and offline. Helped start Poets Union of Australia in the late seventies. Pioneered poetry workshops in Melbourne prisons in the early eighties. Member of 'Word of Mouth' poetry theatre group, mid-eighties. Independent poetry publisher 1982-1992 (proprietor of Abalone Press and member of Pariah Press Cooperative).

Career in librarianship 1962-1980.

Reiki Master, psychic medium, Tarot reader, witch; also studied Druidry, ceremonial magic, Kabbalah.

Born and grew in Launceston, Tasmania. As an adult lived many years in Melbourne; now happily subtropical.

About the Poet: Helen Patrice

Helen Patrice is an Australian neurodiverse writer living in Naarm (Melbourne). She writes speculative and literary poetry, speculative short fiction, creative nonfiction, and memoir. She occasionally blogs at WordPress and SubStack. Her books: *A Woman of Mars*, *Palaentology for Beginners*, *She Too: Four Voice in (Almost) Harmony Three Cycles of the Moon*, *The Communicant and Other Stories*, and *Into Dark Woods* (forthcoming). Her recent publications include *Metonym*, *Pure Slush*, *Lady Liberty*, *Moss Piglet*, *Young Ravens*, *Eye to the Telescope*, and *Fairy Tale Magazine*. Helen takes part in NaNoWriMo most years and has a cache of hidden novels that are hot messes.